Elias Hill

Tiny Camel Books
tinycamelbooks.com
tinycamelbooks@gmail.com

101
So Bad,
They're Good
Dad
Jokes

By: Elias Hill

Illustrations By: Katherine Hogan

What do dyslexic, agnostic, insomniacs do at night?

They stay up wondering if there really is a dog.

Dad, what's the best thing about elevator jokes?

They work on so many levels.

I was just admiring my ceiling.

I know it's not the best ceiling in the world, but it's definitely up there.

What did the data storage company say to the hackers?

Hey! You! Get off of my cloud!

A neutron walks into a bar and asks how much for a drink.

The bartender says, "For you? No charge."

My daughter bet me I couldn't make a car out of spaghetti.

You should've seen the look on her face when I drove pasta.

What did the horse say after he tripped?

"Help, I've fallen and I can't giddy up"

What did the real estate agent say at Thanksgiving?

"This year, I have lots to be thankful for."

Dad, what's a protein?

Someone who advocates for 13-19 year olds.

Dad, what did the Buddhist say to the hot dog vendor?

Make me one with everything.

Inspecting mirrors...

is a job I could really see myself doing.

Dad, how do crazy people get through the forest?

They take the psycho path.

Dad, who does the award for the best neckware go to?

It's a tie.

Dad, how many sodas does it take to give a tropical bird a sugar high?

Toucans.

Dad, what's wrong with ancient history?

We tend to Babylon about it.

Dad, what's a pirate's favorite letter?

You'd think it would be arrrr, but it's actually the "C".

A man took an airline company to court after they lost his luggage.

He also lost his case.

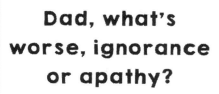

Dad, what did the taxi driver say to the wolf?

Werewolf?

What do you say to someone who has stolen your garden gate?

Nothing because they might take a fence.

I really hate those people who knock at your door and tell you how you need to be 'saved' or you'll 'burn'.

Crazy firemen.

41440816R00059

Made in the USA
Lexington, KY
07 June 2019